foreword

Whether you're looking for hors d'oeuvres for an elegant gathering or munchies for the Saturday night hockey game, a convenient little book of easy dips and spreads always comes in handy. In this collection of popular Company's Coming recipes, you'll find everything from party appetizers to kid-friendly fruit and vegetable dips for healthy after-school snacks.

Amuse your guests by using interesting serving dishes—containers made of food, such as hollowed-out loaves of bread or sweet peppers, are clever dip holders, as are martini glasses or your grandmother's collection of teacups. Try presenting spreads on old records or large ceramic tiles, or serve fruit, veggies or crackers in clean terracotta pots or kids' plastic dump trucks, depending on the occasion. It's all part of the fun when friends and family get together to dip, dunk and dab!

Jean Paré

sun-dried tomato spread

You can store this sweet, tangy tomato and roasted garlic spread in an airtight container in the fridge for up to two days, or in the freezer for up to one month. If it's frozen, let stand at room temperature for 90 minutes to soften.

Garlic bulb	**1**	**1**
Jar of sun-dried tomatoes in oil, drained, coarsely chopped	8 1/2 oz.	251 mL
Block of cream cheese, softened	8 oz.	250 g
Chopped fresh parsley	1/4 cup	60 mL
Lemon juice	2 tbsp.	30 mL
Sweet chili sauce	2 tbsp.	30 mL
Water	2 tbsp.	30 mL
Pepper	1/4 tsp.	1 mL

Trim 1/4 inch (6 mm) from garlic bulb to expose tops of cloves, leaving bulb intact. Wrap loosely in greased foil. Bake in 375°F (190°C) oven for about 45 minutes until softened. Let stand until cool enough to handle. Squeeze garlic bulb to remove cloves from skin. Discard skin. Transfer cloves to blender or food processor.

Add remaining 7 ingredients. Process until smooth. Transfer to small serving bowl. Chill, covered, for 1 hour to blend flavours. Before serving, let stand at room temperature for 30 minutes to soften. Makes about 2 1/4 cups (550 mL).

2 tbsp. (30 mL): 63 Calories; 5.4 g Total Fat (1.7 g Mono, 0.3 g Poly, 3.0 g Sat); 15 mg Cholesterol; 3 g Carbohydrate; trace Fibre; 1 g Protein; 78 mg Sodium

eggplant onion dip

An update on baba ghanouj *(which means 'indulged father' in Arabic), we've sweetened this popular Middle Eastern dip with caramelized onions. Serve with pita bread chips or vegetables.*

Medium eggplants	3	3
Olive (or cooking) oil	3 tbsp.	50 mL
Chopped onion	1 1/2 cups	375 mL
Garlic cloves, minced (or 3/4 tsp., 4 mL, powder)	3	3
Salt	1 tsp.	5 mL
Ground coriander	1/4 tsp.	1 mL
Ground cumin	1/4 tsp.	1 mL
Cayenne pepper	1/8 tsp.	0.5 mL
Chopped fresh parsley	3 tbsp.	50 mL
Lemon juice	2 tbsp.	30 mL
Tahini (sesame paste)	2 tbsp.	30 mL

Poke several holes randomly into each eggplant. Place on foil-lined baking sheet. Bake in 450°F (230°C) oven for about 45 minutes until softened. Let stand for about 10 minutes until cool enough to handle. Cut eggplants in half lengthwise. Discard seeds. Scoop out flesh into food processor. Discard shells. Pulse with on/off motion until finely chopped. Transfer to medium bowl.

Heat olive oil in large frying pan on medium. Add onion and garlic. Cook for 10 to 15 minutes, stirring often, until onion is caramelized. Reduce heat to medium-low.

Add next 4 ingredients. Heat and stir for about 5 minutes until fragrant. Add to eggplant. Stir well.

Add remaining 3 ingredients. Stir well. Chill, covered, for 1 hour to blend flavours. Makes about 2 1/2 cups (625 mL).

2 tbsp. (30 mL): *44 Calories; 2.4 g Total Fat (1.6 g Mono, 0.3 g Poly, 0.3 g Sat); 0 mg Cholesterol; 6 g Carbohydrate; 2 g Fibre; 1 g Protein; 117 mg Sodium*

spicy jalapeño tomato salsa

Packed with flavour and colour, this fabulous salsa makes a wonderful gift as well as an inspired accompaniment to grilled chicken, sausages and steak. Taste it before it's done—if you like extra heat, add more jalapeños.

Medium tomatoes, peeled (see Tip, page 64), and chopped (about 4 lbs., 1.8 kg)	14	14
Large red onion, chopped	1	1
Large green pepper, chopped	1	1
Large red pepper, chopped	1	1
White vinegar	1/2 cup	125 mL
Canned whole pickled jalapeño peppers, drained and chopped (see Tip, page 64)	5	5
Tomato paste (see Tip, page 64)	1/3 cup	75 mL
Brown sugar, packed	3 tbsp.	50 mL
Garlic cloves, minced	6	6
Ground cumin	1 tbsp.	15 mL
Salt	2 tsp.	10 mL

Combine all 11 ingredients in large heavy saucepan. Bring to a boil. Reduce heat to medium. Boil gently, uncovered, for 45 to 50 minutes, stirring occasionally, until thickened. Fill 3 hot sterile pint (500 mL) jars to within 1/2 inch (12 mm) of top. Wipe rims of jars. Place sterile metal lids on jars and screw on metal bands fingertip tight. Do not over-tighten. Process in boiling water bath for 5 minutes (see Note). Remove jars. Cool. Makes about 6 cups (1.5 L).

2 tbsp. (30 mL): 17 Calories; 0.2 g Total Fat (trace Mono, 0.1 g Poly, trace Sat); 0 mg Cholesterol; 4 g Carbohydrate; 1 g Fibre; 1 g Protein; 117 mg Sodium

Note: Processing time is for elevations 1001 to 3000 feet (306 to 915 m) above sea level. Make adjustment for elevation in your area if necessary.

chili cheese bean dip

Unwrap the foil on this heated dip and watch the crowds gather round.
You can add vegetable sticks or crackers to the bread cubes for dipping.

Can of romano beans, rinsed and drained	19 oz.	540 mL
Salsa	1 cup	250 mL
Diced process cheese loaf	3/4 cup	175 mL
Cream cheese, cut up and softened	4 oz.	125 g
Diced green pepper	1/4 cup	60 mL
Sliced green onion	1/4 cup	60 mL
Chili powder	2 tsp.	10 mL
Garlic clove, minced (or 1/4 tsp., 1 mL, powder), optional	1	1
Dried crushed chilies	1/4 tsp.	1 mL
Sourdough bread loaf (about 8 inch, 20 cm, diameter)	1	1
Chopped fresh cilantro (or parsley), optional	2 tsp.	10 mL

Mash beans with fork in large bowl.

Add next 8 ingredients. Stir well.

Cut about 3/4 inch (2 cm) from top of bread loaf. Set aside top. Remove bread from inside of loaf, leaving about 3/4 inch (2 cm) thick shell. Set aside removed bread. Spoon bean mixture into hollowed loaf. Replace top. Wrap loaf in foil. Place on ungreased baking sheet. Bake in 300°F (150°C) oven for about 2 hours until heated through and cheese is melted. Discard foil. Transfer loaf to large serving plate. Remove top of loaf. Cut into bite-sized pieces for dipping.

Sprinkle cilantro over dip. Cut reserved bread into bite-sized pieces for dipping. Arrange around loaf. Makes about 5 cups (1.25 L) dip. Serves 10.

1 serving: 268 Calories; 10.3 g Total Fat (3.1 g Mono, 0.7 g Poly, 5.7 g Sat); 25 mg Cholesterol; 34 g Carbohydrate; 4 g Fibre; 11 g Protein; 778 mg Sodium

bacon and corn dip

A wonderfully smooth dip with the delicious flavours of bacon, sweet corn and creamy cheese. Perfect for raw vegetables or potato chips.

Grated medium Cheddar cheese	1/2 cup	125 mL
Sour cream	1/2 cup	125 mL
Corn relish	1/3 cup	75 mL
Bacon slices, cooked crisp and finely crumbled	4	4
Canned sliced pickled jalapeño pepper, drained and chopped (see Tip, page 64)	1 tbsp.	15 mL

Combine all 5 ingredients in medium microwave-safe bowl. Microwave, uncovered, on medium-high (70%) for 2 to 3 minutes, stirring occasionally, until cheese is melted. Makes about 1 cup (250 mL).

2 tbsp. (30 mL): *78 Calories; 6 g Total Fat (2 g Mono, 0.3 g Poly, 3.3 g Sat); 16 mg Cholesterol; 3 g Carbohydrate; trace Fibre; 3 g Protein; 164 mg Sodium*

green chili dip

Not only an excellent dip but also great as a spread for bagels. Dab a little under cold cuts or cheese slices for extra zip at lunch.

Block of light cream cheese, softened	8 oz.	250 g
Light sour cream	1 cup	250 mL
Can of diced green chilies	4 oz.	113 mL
Minced onion flakes	1 tbsp.	15 mL
Lemon juice	1 tsp.	5 mL
Salt	1/2 tsp.	2 mL
Dry mustard	1/4 tsp.	1 mL

Beat all 7 ingredients in medium bowl until smooth. Chill, covered, for at least 6 hours or overnight to blend flavours. Makes about 2 1/2 cups (625 mL).

2 tbsp. (30 mL): 39 Calories; 3.2 g Total Fat (1.2 g Mono, 0.2 g Poly, 2.4 g Sat); 10 mg Cholesterol; 1 g Carbohydrate; trace Fibre; 2 g Protein; 182 mg Sodium

two-bean dip

Two bean, or not two bean? No need to question this one—it's a winner!
Serve with vegetable crackers or pita chips for a casual gathering or
southwestern potluck.

Can of chickpeas (garbanzo beans), rinsed and drained	19 oz.	540 mL
Can of white kidney beans, rinsed and drained	19 oz.	540 mL
Lemon juice	1/2 cup	125 mL
Garlic cloves, minced (or 3/4 tsp., 4 mL, powder)	3	3
Olive oil	1 tbsp.	15 mL
Salt	1/2 tsp.	2 mL
Drops of hot pepper sauce	4	4
Chopped fresh parsley (or 3/4 tsp., 4 mL, flakes)	1 tbsp.	15 mL

Combine first 7 ingredients in large bowl. Process in 2 batches in blender
or food processor, scraping down side if necessary, until smooth. Transfer
to medium serving bowl.

Add parsley. Stir well. Makes about 3 1/2 cups (875 mL).

2 tbsp. (30 mL): 30 Calories; 0.7 g Total Fat (0.4 g Mono, 0.2 g Poly, 0.1 g Sat);
0 mg Cholesterol; 5 g Carbohydrate; 1 g Fibre; 2 g Protein; 86 mg Sodium

salsa dip

While this can be made up to four days ahead and refrigerated in a covered glass or plastic dish, it can't be frozen. Try it spooned over baked potatoes.

Medium tomatoes, peeled (see Tip, page 64), and diced	3	3
Can of diced green chilies	4 oz.	113 mL
Chopped pitted black olives	1/4 cup	60 mL
Green onions, chopped	3	3
Cooking oil	2 tbsp.	30 mL
White vinegar	1 1/2 tbsp.	25 mL
Garlic powder	1/2 tsp.	2 mL
Salt	1/2 tsp.	2 mL
Pepper	1/8 tsp.	0.5 mL

Combine all 9 ingredients in small bowl. Chill, covered, for at least 2 hours to blend flavours. Makes about 3 cups (750 mL).

2 tbsp. (30 mL): 15 Calories; 1.3 g Total Fat (0.4 g Mono, 0.2 g Poly, 0.1 g Sat); 0 mg Cholesterol; 1 g Carbohydrate; trace Fibre; trace Protein; 64 mg Sodium

kidney bean dip

Some like it hot…so add more cayenne pepper if you like. As a variation, you can substitute black beans for the kidney beans.

BOTTOM LAYER

Cans of kidney beans (14 oz., 398 mL, each), rinsed and drained	2	2
Sliced green onion	1/2 cup	125 mL
Salsa	6 tbsp.	100 mL
Parsley flakes	2 tsp.	10 mL
Chili powder	1 tsp.	5 mL
White vinegar	1 tsp.	5 mL
Onion powder	1/2 tsp.	2 mL
Salt	1/2 tsp.	2 mL
Cayenne pepper	1/4 tsp.	1 mL
Garlic powder	1/4 tsp.	1 mL

TOP LAYER

Grated medium Cheddar cheese	1 cup	250 mL
Grated Monterey Jack cheese	1 cup	250 mL
Chili powder	1 tsp.	5 mL

Bottom Layer: Mash kidney beans with fork in medium bowl.

Add next 9 ingredients. Mix well. Spread in ungreased 9 inch (22 cm) pie plate or shallow baking dish.

Top Layer: Layer all 3 ingredients, in order given, over bottom layer. Bake, uncovered, in 350°F (175°C) oven for 30 minutes until heated through. Makes about 4 cups (1 L).

2 tbsp. (30 mL): 48 Calories; 2.4 g Total Fat (0.7 g Mono, 0.1 g Poly, 1.5 g Sat); 7 mg Cholesterol; 4 g Carbohydrate; 1 g Fibre; 3 g Protein; 158 mg Sodium

spinach dip in a loaf

You can play with this classic dip by putting it into interesting breads—try a sourdough or whole grain loaf.

Box of frozen chopped spinach, thawed and squeezed dry	10 oz.	300 g
Grated Monterey Jack cheese	1 cup	250 mL
Salad dressing (or mayonnaise)	1 cup	250 mL
Sour cream	1 cup	250 mL
Chopped green onion	1/3 cup	75 mL
Envelope of tomato vegetable soup mix	2.5 oz.	71 g
Round (or oblong) bread loaf	1	1

Combine first 6 ingredients in medium bowl.

Cut about 3/4 inch (2 cm) from top of bread loaf. Set aside top. Remove bread from inside of loaf, leaving about 1 inch (2.5 cm) thick shell. Set aside removed bread. Spoon spinach mixture into hollowed loaf. Replace top. Wrap loaf in foil. Place on ungreased baking sheet. Bake in 300°F (150°C) oven for about 2 hours until heated through. Discard foil. Transfer loaf to large serving plate. Remove top of loaf. Cut into bite-sized pieces for dipping. Cut reserved bread into bite-sized pieces for dipping. Arrange around loaf. Makes about 4 cups (1 L) dip. Serves 10.

1 serving: 359 Calories; 20.9 g Total Fat (9.5 g Mono, 4.7 g Poly, 5.7 g Sat); 27 mg Cholesterol; 33 g Carbohydrate; 2 g Fibre; 9 g Protein; 1002 mg Sodium

seafood curry dip

This is a great introduction to Indian food. A hint of curry subtly enhances the mild flavours of shrimp and crabmeat in this not-too-spicy dip. Make it to store in the fridge up to 24 hours ahead so the flavours can mingle.

Cream cheese, softened	1/4 cup	60 mL
Mayonnaise	1/4 cup	60 mL
Finely chopped green onion	2 tbsp.	30 mL
Curry powder	2 tsp.	10 mL
Lime juice	1 1/2 tsp.	7 mL
Coarsely chopped cooked salad shrimp	3/4 cup	175 mL
Can of crabmeat, drained, cartilage removed, flaked	4 1/4 oz.	120 g

Combine first 5 ingredients in large bowl.

Add shrimp and crab. Stir well. Chill, covered, for about 1 hour to blend flavours. Makes about 1 1/3 cups (325 mL).

1 tbsp. (15 mL): 39 Calories; 3.2 g Total Fat (1.5 g Mono, 0.8 g Poly, 0.8 g Sat); 15 mg Cholesterol; trace Carbohydrate; trace Fibre; 2 g Protein; 75 mg Sodium

chili crab dip

The zing of lemon and a little chili heat give this creamy appetizer a pleasant, peppery bite. You can store it in an airtight container in the refrigerator for up to two days.

Block of cream cheese, softened	8 oz.	250 g
Mayonnaise	1/3 cup	75 mL
Lemon juice	3 tbsp.	50 mL
Chopped fresh dill	2 tbsp.	30 mL
Sweet chili sauce	2 tbsp.	30 mL
Salt	1/4 tsp.	1 mL
Pepper	1/4 tsp.	1 mL
Cans of crabmeat (4 1/4 oz., 120 g, each), drained, cartilage removed, flaked	2	2
Chopped fresh chives	2 tbsp.	30 mL

Beat first 7 ingredients in medium bowl until smooth.

Add crab and chives. Stir. Chill, covered, for 1 hour to blend flavours. Makes about 2 2/3 cups (650 mL).

__2 tbsp. (30 mL):__ 137 Calories; 12.6 g Total Fat (4.9 g Mono, 2.0 g Poly, 5.1 g Sat); 27 mg Cholesterol; 2 g Carbohydrate; trace Fibre; 4 g Protein; 312 mg Sodium

crab mousse

A quick spritz of cooking spray will make it easier to remove this mousse from the mold. If you're using a mold with a centre ring, you can place a small cup in the middle to fill with blanched asparagus spears and slices of colourful peppers.

Envelope of unflavoured gelatin (about 1 tbsp., 15 mL)	1/4 oz.	7 g
Cold water	1/4 cup	60 mL
Can of condensed cream of mushroom soup	10 oz.	284 mL
Block of cream cheese, softened	8 oz.	250 g
Salad dressing (or mayonnaise)	2/3 cup	150 mL
Finely chopped celery	3/4 cup	175 mL
Can of crabmeat, drained, cartilage removed, flaked	4 1/4 oz.	120 g
Worcestershire sauce	1 1/2 tsp.	7 mL
Onion flakes	1 tsp.	5 mL

Sprinkle gelatin over cold water in large saucepan. Let stand for 1 minute.

Add next 3 ingredients. Heat and stir on medium until smooth. Remove from heat. Chill until slightly thickened.

Add remaining 4 ingredients. Stir well. Pour into lightly greased 4 cup (1 L) mold. Chill, covered, for at least 1 hour until set. Just before serving, dip mold into warm water to loosen. Invert onto dampened serving plate. Makes about 3 1/2 cups (875 mL).

2 tbsp. (30 mL): 84 Calories; 8.1 g Total Fat (3.4 g Mono, 1.9 g Poly, 2.5 g Sat); 13 mg Cholesterol; 1 g Carbohydrate; trace Fibre; 2 g Protein; 170 mg Sodium

salmon mousse

For smaller gatherings, it's easy to cut this recipe in half. Make sure you make it a few hours ahead of time so it can set.

Envelopes of unflavoured gelatin (1/4 oz., 7 g, each, about 2 tbsp., 30 mL)	2	2
Cold water	1 1/2 cups	375 mL
Low-fat salad dressing (or mayonnaise)	1 cup	250 mL
Fat-free sour cream	1 cup	250 mL
Celery salt	1/2 tsp.	2 mL
Dried dillweed	1/2 tsp.	2 mL
Onion powder	1/2 tsp.	2 mL
Cans of red salmon (7 1/2 oz., 213 g, each), drained, skin and round bones removed, flaked	2	2
Finely chopped English cucumber (with peel)	1 cup	250 mL

Sprinkle gelatin over cold water in small saucepan. Let stand for 1 minute. Heat and stir on low until gelatin is dissolved. Remove from heat. Let stand until cooled, but not thickened.

Combine next 5 ingredients in large bowl. Add gelatin mixture. Stir well. Chill, uncovered, for 1 to 1 1/2 hours, stirring and scraping down sides of bowl occasionally, until slightly thickened.

Fold in salmon and cucumber. Pour into lightly greased 5 cup (1.25 L) mold. Chill, covered, for at least 1 hour until set. Just before serving, dip mold into warm water to loosen. Invert onto dampened serving plate. Makes about 5 cups (1.25 L).

2 tbsp. (30 mL): 62 Calories; 4.7 g Total Fat (1.9 g Mono, 1.1 g Poly, 0 .5 g Sat); 10 mg Cholesterol; 2 g Carbohydrate; trace Fibre; 3 g Protein; 118 mg Sodium

burnt sugar brie

Just three ingredients for this fabulous appetizer! Make the syrup ahead of time and refrigerate up to three months in a sealed container. With a smaller serving dish, drizzle only half the syrup over the cheese and top it up during the evening. Or try a dinner plate and present the Brie in a pool of beautiful, dark sauce.

SUGAR SYRUP

Granulated sugar	1 cup	250 mL
Water	1/2 cup	125 mL
Brie cheese round	4 oz.	125 g

Sugar Syrup: Measure sugar into large frying pan. Heat and stir on medium-low until melted and deep golden in colour. Remove from heat.

Slowly, and very carefully, stir in water. Mixture will sputter furiously and sugar may start to solidify. Heat and stir on medium until sugar is dissolved. Cool. Makes about 2/3 cup (150 mL) syrup.

Place cheese on medium microwave-safe plate. Microwave on high (100%) for 20 to 30 seconds until softened. Pour Sugar Syrup over cheese, allowing it to run down sides. Serves 6.

1 serving: 188 Calories; 5.2 g Total Fat (1.5 g Mono, 0.2 g Poly, 3.3 g Sat); 19 mg Cholesterol; 32 g Carbohydrate; 0 g Fibre; 4 g Protein; 119 mg Sodium

asian cheese spread

This yummy spread takes three days to marinate, but it tastes so good it'll disappear immediately. You can shorten the fridge time to 12 hours (maximum 24 hours) if you slice the cream cheese in half horizontally and then marinate.

Soy sauce	1/2 cup	125 mL
Icing (confectioner's) sugar	1/4 cup	60 mL
Finely chopped green onion	3 tbsp.	50 mL
Minced crystallized ginger	1 1/2 tbsp.	25 mL
Dried crushed chilies	1 tsp.	5 mL
Garlic clove, minced (or 1/4 tsp., 1 mL, powder)	1	1
Block of cream cheese	8 oz.	250 g
Sesame seeds, toasted (see Tip, page 64)	3 tbsp.	50 mL

Put first 6 ingredients into small bowl. Stir until icing sugar is dissolved. Pour into large resealable freezer bag.

Add cream cheese block. Seal bag. Turn until coated. Let stand in refrigerator for 3 days, turning occasionally. Drain.

Put sesame seeds onto large plate. Press both sides of cream cheese block into sesame seeds. Place on serving plate. Sprinkle any remaining sesame seeds over top. Serves 8 to 10.

1 serving: 138 Calories; 12.6 g Total Fat (3.7 g Mono, 1.1 g Poly, 7.1 g Sat); 34 mg Cholesterol; 3 g Carbohydrate; 1 g Fibre; 3 g Protein; 367 mg Sodium

curried onion paneer

Paneer, a fresh and delicate cheese similar in taste to cottage cheese, is used in Indian dishes such as dal, as well as in salads and other vegetable dishes. You'll find it in southeast Asian food stores or even in the freezer section of some grocery stores. Serve with naan or pita bread.

Butter (or hard margarine)	1 tbsp.	15 mL
Chopped onion	1 1/2 cups	375 mL
Dried crushed chilies (optional)	1/8 tsp.	0.5 mL
Brown sugar, packed	1 tbsp.	15 mL
Curry powder	1 tsp.	5 mL
Ground cumin	1/2 tsp.	2 mL
Salt	1/8 tsp.	0.5 mL
Can of diced tomatoes, drained	14 oz.	398 mL
Fresh spinach leaves, lightly packed, cut or torn	1 cup	250 mL
Paneer cheese, cut into 1/4 inch (6 mm) cubes	1/2 lb.	225 g
Lime juice	2 tsp.	10 mL

Sprigs of fresh cilantro (or parsley), for garnish

Melt butter in large frying pan on medium. Add onion and chilies. Cook for 5 to 10 minutes, stirring often, until onion is softened. Reduce heat to medium-low.

Add next 4 ingredients. Stir. Cook for 5 to 10 minutes, stirring occasionally, until onion is caramelized. Increase heat to medium.

Add next 4 ingredients. Stir. Cook for about 10 minutes, stirring occasionally, until spinach is wilted and liquid is evaporated. Transfer to small serving bowl.

Garnish with cilantro. Makes about 3 cups (750 mL).

3 tbsp. (50 mL): 59 Calories; 3.1 g Total Fat (0.9 g Mono, 0.1 g Poly, 1.9 g Sat); 9 mg Cholesterol; 4 g Carbohydrate; 1 g Fibre; 4 g Protein; 140 mg Sodium

curry dip

Great for fresh vegetables, chicken wings, ham cubes and tiny meatballs, this dip is a snap to make.

Light salad dressing (or mayonnaise)	2 cups	500 mL
Ketchup	3 tbsp.	50 mL
Curry powder	1 tbsp.	15 mL
Onion flakes	2 tsp.	10 mL
Granulated sugar	1/2 tsp.	2 mL
White vinegar	1/2 tsp.	2 mL
Cayenne pepper	1/4 tsp.	1 mL
Garlic powder	1/4 tsp.	1 mL

Combine all 8 ingredients in small bowl. Makes about 2 cups (500 mL).

2 tbsp. (30 mL): 92 Calories; 7.7 g Total Fat (4.4 g Mono, 2.2 g Poly, 0.4 g Sat); 0 mg Cholesterol; 6 g Carbohydrate; trace Fibre; trace Protein; 267 mg Sodium

sardine lemon spread

A quick and easy, fresh-tasting spread to delight your taste buds. Add more lemon juice and chili paste if you'd like, and serve with toasted tortilla wedges or crusty bread.

Cans of sardines (7 1/2 oz., 206 g, each), drained	2	2
Chopped fresh parsley	3 tbsp.	50 mL
Lemon juice	1 tbsp.	15 mL
Chili paste (sambal oelek)	1/2 tsp.	2 mL
Salt	1/4 tsp.	1 mL
Pepper	1/8 tsp.	0.5 mL

Put sardines into medium bowl. Break into small pieces with fork.

Add remaining 5 ingredients. Mix well. Makes about 1 cup (250 mL).

1 tbsp. (15 mL): 26 Calories; 1.4 g Total Fat (0.5 g Mono, 0.6 g Poly, 0.2 g Sat); 17 mg Cholesterol; trace Carbohydrate; trace Fibre; 3 g Protein; 97 mg Sodium

blue cheesecake

It's the blue cheese ingredient that gives this recipe it's name. Serve this as a spread at a party, or as wedges for the first course of a sit-down dinner, garnished with sour cream. Make it 24 hours ahead of time to free up your big day.

Fine dry bread crumbs	2 tbsp.	30 mL
Grated Parmesan cheese	1 tbsp.	15 mL
Bacon slices, diced	8	8
Finely chopped onion	1 cup	250 mL
Blocks of cream cheese (8 oz., 250 g, each), softened	3	3
Blue cheese, crumbled	4 oz.	113 g
Large eggs	4	4
Sour cream	1/2 cup	125 mL
Hot pepper sauce	1/4 tsp.	1 mL

Combine bread crumbs and Parmesan cheese in small bowl. Grease bottom and side of 9 inch (22 cm) springform pan. Sprinkle with crumb mixture. Turn pan to coat bottom and side. Gently tap to remove excess crumb mixture. Set aside.

Heat large frying pan on medium. Add bacon and onion. Cook for about 10 minutes, stirring often, until bacon is crisp. Drain.

Beat cream cheese, blue cheese and 1 egg in medium bowl until smooth. Little bits of blue cheese will remain. Add remaining eggs, 1 at a time, beating well after each addition.

Add sour cream. Beat well. Add hot pepper sauce and bacon mixture. Stir. Pour into prepared pan. Spread evenly. Bake in 325°F (160°C) oven for 1 to 1 1/2 hours until centre is almost set. Run knife around inside edge of pan to allow cheesecake to settle evenly. Let stand in pan on wire rack until cooled completely. Chill, covered, for at least 6 hours or overnight. Cuts into 20 thin wedges.

1 wedge: 197 Calories; 17.9 g Total Fat (5.4 g Mono, 0.9 g Poly, 10.6 g Sat); 93 mg Cholesterol; 3 g Carbohydrate; trace Fibre; 7 g Protein; 255 mg Sodium

cheese log

Make this for the day's events or freeze for just-in-case. Save rolling it in parsley or chopped nuts until after the log has thawed in the refrigerator for eight hours.

Grated Edam (or Gouda) cheese	2 cups	500 mL
Fat-free sour cream	2/3 cup	150 mL
Prepared mustard	1 tsp.	5 mL
Worcestershire sauce	1/4 tsp.	1 mL

**Parsley flakes (or chopped nuts),
   for coating (optional)**

Put first 4 ingredients into medium bowl. Mash with fork until smooth. Roll into log.

Roll log in parsley on large plate until coated. Chill, covered, until ready to serve. Makes about 1 1/4 cups (300 mL).

1 tbsp. (15 mL): 51 Calories; 3.8 g Total Fat (1.1 g Mono, 0.1 g Poly, 2.4 g Sat); 12 mg Cholesterol; 1 g Carbohydrate; trace Fibre; 4 g Protein; 140 mg Sodium

creamy cheese dip

The addition of beer gives this cheesy dip a unique, zippy flavour. Great with nacho chips and, well, beer! If the food processor's on the blink, just mash the ingredients with a fork.

Block of cream cheese, softened	8 oz.	250 g
Grated medium Cheddar cheese	2/3 cup	150 mL
Beer	1/4 cup	60 mL
Chopped green onion	2 tbsp.	30 mL
Worcestershire sauce	2 tsp.	10 mL

Thinly sliced green onion, for garnish

Process first 5 ingredients in food processor until smooth. Transfer to small bowl. Chill, covered, for 2 to 3 hours to blend flavours. Let stand at room temperature for 30 minutes before serving.

Garnish with green onion. Makes about 1 2/3 cups (400 mL).

2 tbsp. (30 mL): 89 Calories; 8.2 g Total Fat (2.3 g Mono, 0.3 g Poly, 5.2 g Sat); 26 mg Cholesterol; 1 g Carbohydrate; trace Fibre; 3 g Protein; 98 mg Sodium

a dipper's dip

Intense yellow colour with green flecks. Serve this tangy dip with assorted chips.

Light mayonnaise	1/2 cup	125 mL
Light sour cream	1/2 cup	125 mL
Prepared mustard	1/4 cup	60 mL
Dried dillweed	2 tsp.	10 mL
Prepared horseradish	2 tsp.	10 mL
Garlic powder	1/4 tsp.	1 mL

Combine all 6 ingredients in small bowl. Chill, covered, for 1 hour to blend flavours. Makes about 1 1/2 cups (375 mL).

2 tbsp. (30 mL): 45 Calories; 4.1 g Total Fat (2.3 g Mono, 1.2 g Poly, 1.1 g Sat); 2 mg Cholesterol; 2 g Carbohydrate; trace Fibre; 1 g Protein; 140 mg Sodium

best vegetable dip

Freeze half of this large recipe for up to six months so you have a sweet veggie dip at your fingertips. For a slightly paler dip, you can substitute light corn syrup for dark.

Block of cream cheese, softened	8 oz.	250 g
Dark corn syrup	1/2 cup	125 mL
Granulated sugar	1/2 cup	125 mL
Cooking oil	1 cup	250 mL
Minced onion flakes	1/4 cup	60 mL
White vinegar	1/4 cup	60 mL
Lemon juice	1 tbsp.	15 mL
Celery seed	1 tsp.	5 mL
Dry mustard	1 tsp.	5 mL
Salt	1/2 tsp.	2 mL
Paprika	1/4 tsp.	1 mL

Beat first 3 ingredients in medium bowl until smooth.

Add cooking oil. Stir well.

Add remaining 7 ingredients. Beat well. Chill, covered, until ready to serve. Makes about 3 cups (750 mL).

2 tbsp. (30 mL): 156 Calories; 12.8 g Total Fat (6.5 g Mono, 2.9 g Poly, 2.9 g Sat); 11 mg Cholesterol; 11 g Carbohydrate; trace Fibre; 1 g Protein; 86 mg Sodium

creamy ham ball

This lovely pink spread doesn't need a coating. Serve with assorted crackers. Make ahead and refrigerate, covered, for up to two days, or freeze.

Cans of flaked ham (6 1/2 oz., 184 g, each), drained and broken up	2	2
Block of cream cheese, softened	8 oz.	250 g
Chopped chives	1 tbsp.	15 mL
Light salad dressing (or mayonnaise)	1 tbsp.	15 mL
Parsley flakes	2 tsp.	10 mL
Cayenne pepper	1/4 tsp.	1 mL
Dry mustard	1/4 tsp.	1 mL

Put all 7 ingredients into medium bowl. Mix well. Shape into ball. Makes about 1 2/3 cups (400 mL).

1 tbsp. (15 mL): 81 Calories; 7.3 g Total Fat (2.7 g Mono, 0.5 g Poly, 3.5 g Sat); 21 mg Cholesterol; trace Carbohydrate; trace Fibre; 4 g Protein; 265 mg Sodium

herb spread

One taste and you'll be hooked! Delicious on crackers or crusty bread.

Block of cream cheese, cut up and softened	8 oz.	250 g
Chopped fresh chives	3 tbsp.	50 mL
Finely chopped fresh parsley	3 tbsp.	50 mL
Pepper	1 tsp.	5 mL
Sweet chili sauce	2 tbsp.	30 mL
Soy sauce	1 tbsp.	15 mL

Chopped fresh chives, for garnish
Finely chopped fresh parsley, for garnish

Beat cream cheese in medium bowl until smooth.

Add next 3 ingredients. Beat well.

Add chili sauce and soy sauce. Beat well. Chill, covered, for at least 2 hours to blend flavours.

Garnish with second amount of chives and second amount of parsley. Makes about 1 1/4 cups (300 mL).

1 tbsp. (15 mL): 46 Calories; 4.3 g Total Fat (1.2 g Mono, 0.2 g Poly, 2.7 g Sat); 14 mg Cholesterol; 1 g Carbohydrate; trace Fibre; 1 g Protein; 112 mg Sodium

sweet ginger spread

Crystallized ginger, a popular treat on its own, melds seamlessly with other traditional Asian ingredients in this easy spread. Serve with rice crackers and crisp vegetables. You can also shape the mixture into a ball, refrigerate until firm and then roll in toasted black and white sesame seeds before serving.

Block of cream cheese, softened	8 oz.	250 g
Sweet chili sauce	2 tbsp.	30 mL
Minced crystallized ginger	1 1/2 tbsp.	25 mL
Finely chopped green onion	1 tbsp.	15 mL
Lime juice	2 tsp.	10 mL
Grated lime zest	1/2 tsp.	2 mL
Finely chopped green onion	1/2 tsp.	2 mL
Sesame seeds, toasted (see Tip, page 64)	1/2 tsp.	2 mL

Beat first 6 ingredients in medium bowl until well mixed. Chill, covered, for at least 6 hours or overnight to blend flavours.

Sprinkle with second amount of green onion and sesame seeds. Makes about 1 1/3 cups (325 mL).

1 tbsp. (15 mL): 43 Calories; 4.0 g Total Fat (1.1 g Mono, 0.2 g Poly, 2.5 g Sat); 12 mg Cholesterol; 1 g Carbohydrate; trace Fibre; 1 g Protein; 55 mg Sodium

fluffy peach dip

This delicately flavoured dip with the consistency of soft whipped cream goes perfectly with fresh fruit.

Liquid whip topping	1 cup	250 mL
Peach jelly powder (gelatin)	1 tbsp.	15 mL
Vanilla extract	1/2 tsp.	2 mL
Peach yogurt	3/4 cup	175 mL

Beat first 3 ingredients in medium bowl for about 5 minutes until soft peaks form.

Add yogurt. Beat well. Makes about 3 1/2 cups (875 mL).

2 tbsp. (30 mL): 25 Calories; 1.6 g Total Fat (trace Mono, 0 g Poly, 0.1 g Sat); trace Cholesterol; 2 g Carbohydrate; 0 g Fibre; trace Protein; 4 mg Sodium

easy fruit dip

Terrific at a party for adults or kids, this also makes a healthy dessert drizzled over slices of in-season fruit.

Plain yogurt	1 cup	250 mL
Icing (confectioner's) sugar	3 tbsp.	50 mL
Grated lemon zest	1/2 tsp.	2 mL

Combine all 3 ingredients in small bowl. Makes about 1 cup (250 mL).

2 tbsp. (30 mL): 30 Calories; 0.5 g Total Fat (0.1 g Mono, trace Poly, 0.3 g Sat); 2 mg Cholesterol; 5 g Carbohydrate; trace Fibre; 2 g Protein; 22 mg Sodium

peanut butter dip

Even youngsters can whip this up, and it's great with fruit as an after-school snack.

Smooth peanut butter	1/2 cup	125 mL
Orange juice	3 tbsp.	50 mL
Corn syrup	1 1/2 tbsp.	25 mL
Frozen whipped topping, thawed	1 cup	250 mL

Combine first 3 ingredients in small bowl.

Fold in whipped topping until just combined. Makes about 1 1/3 cups (325 mL).

1 tbsp. (15 mL): 53 Calories; 4 g Total Fat (1.6 g Mono, 0.9 g Poly, 1.4 g Sat); 0 mg Cholesterol; 3 g Carbohydrate; trace Fibre; 2 g Protein; 31 mg Sodium

recipe index

topical tips

Chopping jalapeño peppers: Wear protective gloves when handling jalapeño peppers. Do not touch your face near eyes.

To peel tomatoes: Cut an 'X' on the bottom of each tomato, just through the skin. Place tomatoes in boiling water for 30 seconds. Immediately transfer to a bowl of ice water. Let stand until cool enough to handle. Peel and discard skins.

Toasting nuts, seeds or coconut: Cooking times will vary for each type of nut—so never toast them together. For small amounts, place ingredient in an ungreased shallow frying pan. Heat on medium for three to five minutes, stirring often, until golden. For larger amounts, spread ingredient evenly in an ungreased shallow pan. Bake in 350°F (175°C) oven for five to 10 minutes, stirring or shaking often, until golden.

Tomato paste leftovers: If a recipe calls for less than an entire can of tomato paste, freeze the unopened can for 30 minutes. Open both ends and push the contents through one end. Slice off only what you need. Freeze the remaining paste in a resealable freezer bag or plastic wrap for future use.

Nutrition Information Guidelines

Each recipe is analyzed using the Canadian Nutrient File from Health Canada, which is based on the United States Department of Agriculture (USDA) Nutrient Database.

- If more than one ingredient is listed (such as "butter or hard margarine"), or if a range is given (1 – 2 tsp., 5 – 10 mL), only the first ingredient or first amount is analyzed.

- For meat, poultry and fish, the serving size per person is based on the recommended 4 oz. (113 g) uncooked weight (without bone), which is 2 – 3 oz. (57 – 85 g) cooked weight (without bone)— approximately the size of a deck of playing cards.

- Milk used is 1% M.F. (milk fat), unless otherwise stated.

- Cooking oil used is canola oil, unless otherwise stated.

- Ingredients indicating "sprinkle," "optional" or "for garnish" are not included in the nutrition information.

- The fat in recipes and combination foods can vary greatly depending on the sources and types of fats used in each specific ingredient. For these reasons, the count of saturated, monounsaturated and polyunsaturated fats may not Add up to the total fat content.